The Windmill Co

Green's Mill, Nottingham	3
Baking in my Family	4
Baking Wholemeal Bread	6
Baking for the Family	17
Festive Fare	22
Use Your Oats	29
Roly Poly, Pudding & Pie	37
Baking for Special Occasions	40
Salt Dough Modelling	45
Conversions: Metric & Imperial	47

© D Metcalf 1993
Published by City of Nottingham
Department of Leisure and Community Services 1993
Reprinted 1996

ISBN 0 905634 27 6

Green's Mill

GREEN'S MILL, NOTTINGHAM

Green's Mill is a restored working tower windmill near the centre of Nottingham. It was built in the year 1807 by Mr Green, a Nottingham baker and was later owned and operated by his son, George.

George Green was a most remarkable man for, as well as being a hard working miller, he was also an outstanding mathematician and theoretical physicist. The mathematical techniques he devised, known to this day as Green's Theorem and Green's Functions, are now used by scientists throughout the world in almost every branch of the physical sciences and engineering.

After milling for about 60 years, the mill ceased work in the mid-1860s and for another five decades or more was left to decay. Its fortunes revived a little in the early 1920s when the mill was used for the manufacture of furniture polish. Alas in 1947 the mill caught fire and was completely gutted, only the brick tower remained standing. Again the mill was left derelict.

Because of the association of the mill with the mathematician George Green, members of the Nottingham University departments of Physics and Mathematics, supported by the local community, raised the money to buy the mill tower. In 1979 they presented it to the City of Nottingham who restored the mill to working order.

Visitors can often see the windmill at work and can buy stoneground flour and oatmeal. The adjacent Centre tells the remarkable story of George Green and his mill.

Dorothy Metcalf, one of our staff at the Mill, has introduced many people – children and adults – to the joys of baking delicious bread, cakes and pastries with Green's Mill wholemeal flour. For each of her very popular workshops Dorothy produced a recipe leaflet with many useful and interesting ideas for things to bake. In response to many requests she has collected them together into this book.

Each of these recipes has been tried and tested at Green's Mill. We hope that you enjoy baking – and eating – them as much as we have.

Denny Plowman
Keeper of Green's Mill

BAKING IN MY FAMILY

As a teenager in 1947 I started work on the opposite side of the River Trent from Sneinton, where the sadly dilapidated tower of George Green's windmill stood. The mill had suffered the ravages of a disastrous fire in July of that year, just two months before I realised that Nottingham had ever had any windmills at all! Little did I imagine that I would be lucky enough to work at the now splendidly restored and working windmill.

In the early 1920s my mother, still in her teens, had taken the responsibility for the care of her father and eight brothers and sisters on her mother's death. Her father and five of her brothers were colliers in a South Yorkshire mine and she

catered for the family's bread needs by a routine of baking three times each week. Each batch used 1½ stones (21lbs or 9½kgs) of stoneground flour and over a gallon of water, mixed in a very large earthenware panchion. These vessels were hand thrown like a huge, wide plant pot, cream glazed on the inside and with a thicker roll of clay around the top to strengthen the rim.

My mother was only just over five feet tall and found a table too high to knead the dough, so she stood the panchion on a kitchen chair. Eventually its thickened edge wore through the staves and the chair back fell off.

The risen dough was shaped into large loaves and nine at a time were baked in the oven of a wide Yorkshire range, heated by a coal fire. The remainder of the large mix of dough would make bread cobs to eat fresh and warm and maybe a lardy cake or spiced fruit loaf. The bread loaves were not cut into on the day they were made, needing time to 'settle'.

The miller regularly delivered the stoneground wholemeal flour in large returnable cotton sacks and it was stored in a special wooden box in the kitchen. Each sack held one hundredweight (112lbs or over

COTTAGE LOAF.

50kgs), enough for two weeks supply of bread. But that was not the full baking story; consider the pies, puddings, scones and cakes needed to keep this large, hard working family well fed.

When my mother married and had her own family it was natural for her to continue the tradition started in her mother's kitchen and we hardly ate other than home made bread, pies and cakes.

Thank goodness I don't have to clean the flues, make sure the chimney is swept and get a good bright fire before I can bake at home. Many of the old ways have been overtaken by improved techniques and ingredients. We have soft margarines and vegetable oil to replace lard and suet. High quality cleaned, dried fruits and nuts may be had in great variety, as can flavourings, seasonings, herbs and spices unknown to previous generations. Our blenders, mixers and food processors relieve us of a lot of the hard work of preparation.

However, I believe that the 'hands-on' activity of kneading and shaping bread dough is something that won't be replaced as a basic and therapeutic exercise. And have you ever heard anyone say: 'I don't like the smell or taste of home made bread?'

Working at a windmill where we sell stoneground meals made from British wheat and oats, I regard the promotion of these products as important in furthering interest in the Centre's other attractions to visitors. Many people who have been disappointed with the results of previous efforts at bread making have been to sessions at the windmill and have learned a few tips to be more successful. With the idea of 'catching them young' groups of children have also come and baked bread at Green's Mill.

Do not be afraid to try it. Although today's bread baking might seem more sophisticated, the consistent quality of the ingredients ensures success. What has not changed is the untampered taste and nutritional value that results from using fresh stoneground wholemeal flour. Green's Mill flour can be used in any of your own wholemeal recipes; many of those in this book are adaptations of my own Family Favourites.

Dorothy Metcalf

BAKING WHOLEMEAL BREAD

Ingredients

Flour

The quality of the flour is important when making bread. 'Strong' wheat flours have a high protein content that, when mixed with water, forms gluten. It is this strong, continuous web of elastic gluten which holds the aerating gases as bubbles in the dough.

Flours made from other grains and seeds may be used in bread and will give an interesting variety to your baking. However, rye, barley, oats, maize and buckwheat, for instance, have less gluten than wheat so slight modifications to your recipes and techniques may be necessary. Substitute 2oz (50gm) of these unusual flours in every 1lb (500gm) of wheat flour to start with and go on from there.

You will give the dough a good start in cold weather if you warm the mixing bowl and flour first. Rest the bowl of flour over a pan of hot water for 10 minutes or warm on medium power in a microwave oven for half a minute.

Store all flours in a cool, dry place away from strong smelling foods.

Yeast

In the past the only type of yeast available was a liquid 'barm', a by-product of the brewing undertaken at home. It was kept by the housewife as a live culture, cherished with a warm environment and fed at regular intervals with fresh flour, warm water and a pinch of sugar. Part of this culture was used to make a fresh batch of bread and a piece of the resulting dough stirred back into the stock culture, always hoping to keep the yeast strong and robust from the wild yeast spores on the fresh flour. Good 'barm' might be traded with a neighbour and the resulting hybrid could be better than either parent. However, these wild yeasts were inconvenient and could be unreliable and temperamental, sometimes producing heavy and unpalatable bread. Perhaps this is why baking with yeast acquired the reputation of being difficult and surrounded by mystique.

Today we have the benefit of several different kinds of modern yeast. In choosing the one most convenient for you, following these tips will help you to be successful.

Fresh Yeast

Fresh yeast looks rather like putty and is sold by many supermarkets and wholefood shops. It needs to be started into growth with a little of the warm water in the recipe and just a pinch of sugar (before you mix in the flour and the salt). Leave in a warm place for about 15 minutes for it to become frothy before mixing the yeast into dough with the rest of the liquid.

Dried Yeast

Dried yeast is available in several different kinds, most of which are sold vacuum packed in sachets so that they have a long shelf life. They are very convenient to keep in stock, ready to use at short notice. The technique for using dried yeast depends upon which type you have: be careful to read the instructions.

Granular dried yeast is used like fresh yeast, being activated with some of the warm liquid and a pinch of sugar and set to froth before being added to the rest of the ingredients.

'Easy-blend' yeast saves a good deal of time as you don't have to start it into growth. It is mixed with the dry flour before adding any liquid at all. In fact it will fail miserably if you set it to work first with water. The handling of the dough, kneading, rising and proving all proceed as if you were using fresh yeast. At least one brand of Easy-blend yeast contains a little vitamin C that speeds up the growth of the yeast. With this type of 'Fast Action' Easy-blend yeast the dough requires only one rising, in the tins, so you can be baking your bread within an hour! One 6-7gm sachet will raise 1½lb (750gm) of flour.

With practice you will be able to use almost double the weight of flour yet still using only a half to one ounce (15-30gm) of fresh yeast: the less yeast used, the better the bread! It is by no means an exact science and the fact that twice as much flour is used does not mean that double the yeast is required; just as long as you are willing to allow the dough a little more time to rise. Commercial processes for bulk bread making may use as much as twenty times more yeast than you would use at home, a third more water plus the mis-named 'improvers'. This may partly explain the difference between bakers' and home-made bread.

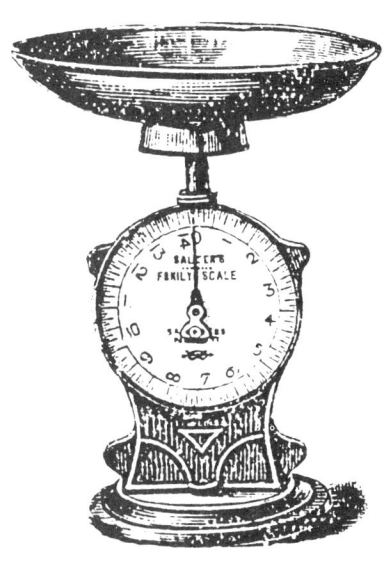

Salt

Salt is an important ingredient, not only for its flavour but for its action as a regulator of the growth of the yeast. In slow rising dough it prevents the fermentation becoming sour, a cause of loaves with poor volume and shape. Salt retards the action of the yeast and indeed will kill it if sprinkled directly onto the fresh yeast, so blend the salt thoroughly into the dry flour before starting to make the dough, regardless of whether you are using fresh or dried yeast. If you like to use crystal salt it is best to dissolve it first in a little of the warm water used in the recipe as the coarse particles may not fully break down during kneading. A good rule of thumb is to use a level teaspoon of salt per 1lb (500gm) of flour.

Liquid

The liquid, usually water, for mixing the dough should be comfortably warm. Mixing two measures of cold water with one of boiling water will give the correct temperature. If the liquid is cooler the dough will still rise but will take longer. If the water is too hot you risk killing the yeast and the dough will not rise. You will need half a pint (300ml) of liquid to every 1lb (500gm) of flour. Adding a little milk or plain yoghurt as part of the liquid enriches the bread and makes a softer crust. A teaspoon of plain malt extract or honey stirred into the liquid helps the yeast to become active quickly.

Method

You will find it best to add nearly all the liquid at once when you start to mix the dough. If it is slightly sticky when you begin to knead it is easier to add a little flour, rather than try to moisten a large lump of stiff, dryish dough.

Kneading

This is the process of mixing the dough into a smooth consistent mass with no streaks of dry flour or surplus liquid. As the gluten forms during the kneading the feel of the dough will change, becoming pliable and rubbery. Pull and stretch the dough, working on a flat surface so that you can turn and push strongly. You will develop a rhythm that is comfortable and which can be quite therapeutic! Test the dough by pressing in a finger to make a dent: if the mark comes out quickly it is kneaded sufficiently. Some experts suggest that if you knead longer than is necessary the sharp bran particles in wholemeal flour tear the gluten as it forms, reducing its strength and raising power and causing the bread to be heavy.

Rising

This is the first part of the yeast's growth through the doughy mass. The fermentation produces carbon dioxide that aerates the dough and it should double in size. Prevent a dry skin forming on the dough by rolling it round in a lightly oiled bowl, cover with polythene and a clean tea towel and put in a warm place to rise. Do not be tempted to hurry this part of the process by putting it too near a heat source; uneven or 'one-sided' heat will cause dry, hard patches in the developing dough and the bread will stale quickly. A warm airing cupboard, living room temperature or a sunny window sill will be fine. If it suits your timetable better, leave it overnight in a cool place such as the pantry or even in the garage! If you rise it in a cool place it will need bringing to room temperature before you can shape it. It is ready to shape into loaves when a finger dent won't recover quickly.

Knocking Back

This is simply a matter of smacking the risen dough down with the back of your hand. The rise will collapse, flattening the large spaces previously filled with the aerating gases that will escape. If you wish at this stage you can lightly mould the dough into a ball and let it rise again. This second rising will be quicker than the first and will produce a well-ripened dough, resulting in loaves of even texture and a sweet mature flavour.

Shaping

Cut the risen dough into pieces of a size to two-thirds fill your chosen baking tins, which should be lightly greased and warm. Using the least flour necessary on your working surface flatten the portion into an oblong as long as the tin and three times as wide. Roll up Swiss roll fashion or fold 'sides to middle' and place the dough, join downwards, in the tin. Tuck in the ends and press out to fill the corners well.

For baps and rolls shape the dough into smooth balls and place them, not quite touching, on warm, greased baking sheets. Decorative shapes are easily achieved such as knots, twists, clover leaves, plaits and small cottage loaves.

Proving the Dough

This is the last part of the preparation before you bake the dough. During this time the dough will recover and grow again, 'proving' that the yeast is still alive and active. Cover the tins with polythene and set in a warm place to allow the dough to rise again and fill the tin. Protect it from draughts as this is the only time that the dough is fragile and susceptible to shock. The pieces should

once more rise to about double in size. If the worst happens and the dough rises too much and sags in the tins, tip the pieces out, gently reshape them, replace in the tins and allow them to prove again.

Finishes

You may add a finish after shaping the dough or during the proof. Brush the shapes with milk, egg wash, salted water or light syrup for sweet breads. Poppy, sesame or cumin seeds or kibbled wheat give a crunchy bite. If you decorate the tops of the loaves with cuts or slashes the cuts will open out, giving an extra area of crust. Use a really sharp knife or you will flatten the proof; a 'Stanley' or other craft knife, kept specially for kitchen use, is ideal.

Baking

When you can see that the dough is rising well during the proof and developing a nicely domed top, put the oven on to pre-heat. Yeast dough requires a really 'bold' start to kill the yeast as quickly as possible. This prevents large holes forming in the crumb or 'flying crust' where the top crust lifts off.

Bake at 220°C (450°F, Reg 7-8) for the first 10-15 minutes for loaves and then reduce to 200°C (400°F, Reg 6-7) for the rest of the baking time. Rolls take only 15-20 minutes total cooking time, loaves 30-50 minutes depending on size. If you are using a fan assisted oven reduce these temperatures by 10-20°C.

The loaves will have shrunk slightly from the tins when they are cooked, with the crust well-formed and brown. When removed from the tins and tapped underneath the loaves will give a hollow ring, rather than a thud! For a crisper crust put them back onto the oven shelves out of their tins for a few extra minutes.

Always cool the bread on wire racks or the condensed steam will make the loaves heavy.

WHOLEMEAL BREAD

1½lb (750g) of wholemeal flour
generous teaspoon salt
pinch of brown sugar
about ¾ pint (400ml) warm water
2 teaspoons fresh yeast (or dried yeast of your choice)

Dissolve the fresh yeast in about half a tea cupful of the warm water, add a pinch only of sugar and allow it to become frothy. Mix the warmed flour with the salt in a warmed bowl, make a well in the centre and pour in the frothy yeast and the remainder of the water. Gradually stir all together with a knife to make a scone-like dough and then knead until the texture becomes smooth and elastic. A little more flour may be necessary if the dough is sticky.

You need not follow bread recipes slavishly so far as precise weights are concerned. The type of wheat milled, the freshness of the flour and the weather conditions will all cause variations. Follow the previous directions for rising, shaping and baking the dough. The quantities given will make one small loaf (about 1lb of risen dough) plus about eight dinner rolls.

Variations upon a Theme

Many ingredients may be introduced to add variety to your bread. Kibbled wheat (crushed, rather than ground, grains) gives a rough, nutty texture if included as part of the flour. The broken grains will soften if soaked overnight in some of the water to be used in the bread. Add a teaspoon of malt extract to give a passable imitation of Granary flour. Soya flour, made from soya beans, is high in protein and makes a nutritious addition to your bread. 'Jumbo' rolled grain flakes can be used in the same way as kibbled wheat; try oats, barley or rye. Children will enjoy making Breakfast Cereal bread by adding crushed Weetabix, Shredded Wheat, cornflakes and any other cereals to the flour.

Problems with your bread?

The protein 'gluten' is the dough's 'skeleton'; the strength of the bread dough depends upon the gluten's elasticity which enables the dough to rise. High protein 'strong' flours make the best bread. The gluten may be softened by being too warm, by using too much yeast or by the addition of fats, sugar or malt to the recipe, so you may need to allow the dough longer to rise.

The bran and wheatgerm enzymes in wholemeal flour may also retard the rising. You can strengthen the gluten by adding sufficient salt to assist the fermenting action, by using an acidic liquid to make the dough (by adding a little plain yoghurt, buttermilk, tomato juice, lemon juice or ascorbic acid – vitamin C) and by quick and vigorous kneading and a thorough knocking back after the first rise. If you are using a low protein flour replace some of that in the recipe with some semolina. Above all do not rush the rise.

Troubleshooting

Bread is 'close' with a heavy crumb?
- yeast insufficient or not active
- the dough was too dry
- the rise and proof too short
- too hot an oven at the start, setting the crust hard

Big holes in the loaf?
- these are produced in the first rising: be sure to knock back the dough before shaping and proving.

Bread dries out quickly?
- rising time too short
- dough mixed too 'tight' (dry)
- flour low in gluten
- rise and proof too warm

Bread crumb sticky?
- dough too 'slack' (wet)
- dough over proved
- too short a baking time

FANCY BREAD FROM PLAIN DOUGH

Plain bread dough may be used in a similar way to pastry to produce scrumptious home-made savoury or sweet 'goodies'. The raising power of the yeast gives a light, rich taste without having to use too much fat or sugar. They are good to eat fresh or may be frozen to eat later and they re-heat well. If you prepare packed lunches, yeast dough is not so fragile as pastry and it is more satisfying, especially if made with wholemeal flour!

PIZZA

Keep the topping ingredients simple – don't be tempted to use up all the leftovers in the refrigerator.

Pat out a portion of the risen dough into a circle on a greased sheet, making the dough about half an inch thick at the centre with a slightly thicker rim around the edge. If you like the flavour of olive oil brush the surface with about one tablespoonful – or your own choice of oil. Have all the ingredients for the topping ready; if you are using onion, peppers or bacon they should be finely sliced and lightly cooked first. Tomatoes are better if the juice is drained off; the topping should not be sloppy.

Variations on the toppings might include:
- tomato with grated cheese.
- finely sliced and softened onion with tomato and cheese.
- flaked tuna and sweetcorn
- sliced mushrooms with flaked, smoked mackerel.

Sprinkle the top with herbs – oregano is good with tomato – plus a little coarse salt and black pepper. Olives and anchovies give an authentic Mediterranean flavour to a tomato pizza.

Leave the pizza to prove for about 10 minutes and then bake at 220°C (425°F, Reg 7) for 15 minutes then lower the heat to 190°C (375°F, Reg 5) for a further 10 minutes.

PITTA BREAD

Pittas make an interesting change from ordinary baps. Filled with thinly sliced meat, flaked fish or grated cheese with a generous salad garnish these warm bread pouches make a nutritious lunch or supper.

Pittas are made from large egg-sized pieces of ordinary bread dough. Roll them out on a floured surface to an oval shape no more than ½" thick and about 6" (15cm) long, cover and allow them to rise in a warm place for 20 minutes or so. Meanwhile preheat the oven with the greased baking sheets inside to 230°C (450°F, Reg 8). Place the risen pittas on the hot baking sheets and cook for 5-6 minutes; don't over-bake. Some of the pittas will be puffy and brown. When you wish to use them preheat the grill and cook the pittas for about 2 minutes on both sides. Beware: they will quickly scorch if your attention wanders! Take great care of the steam when you split them open ready for their fillings.

FOLDED SAVOURY SLICES

Instead of making round, open pizzas, you can roll out the risen dough into an oblong, spread two-thirds of the surface with the savoury ingredients and flip the plain third over and over again to enclose the filling. Press the 'seams' together and gently flatten it out to fill an oblong baking tin of suitable size. Being folded the dough is thicker and needs to prove and recover its 'puffiness'. Then, with a very sharp knife, cut right through into portions so that when baked they can be broken apart. These pieces have the filling enclosed which makes them neater to pack into a lunch box or to serve at a buffet. Before baking the top may be brushed with an egg and milk wash and sprinkled with poppy or sesame seeds. Grated cheese on top gives a tasty finish. Bake at 220°C (425°F, Reg 7) for 20-25 minutes. Allow to cool for a few minutes in the tin then turn out onto a wire rack.

SWEET CAKES

A quick way to make sweet dough cakes is to use the method for the

savoury slices. Roll out, not too thinly, a portion of the risen dough into an oblong. Spread two-thirds of the surface with soft margarine. Fold and turn the dough and roll out and repeat with the margarine once again, using about 1oz (25g) each time. This makes the finished pieces quite flaky.

A variety of fillings may then be used to flavour the cakes, such as:
- sultanas with finely chopped cooking apples.
- chopped dates, softened in a little water, with lemon juice and nutmeg.
- apricot or plum jam with chopped nuts or ground almonds.

Spiced Sugar

Stir together a little Demerara sugar with a good pinch of mixed spice, ground ginger or cinnamon and sprinkle over the filling. This trick distributes the spice very evenly, instead of in lumps!

CHELSEA BUNS

A quick way of making Chelsea Buns is to roll out the risen dough into an oblong, spread all over with softened margarine and a mixture of dried fruit, candied peel and 'spiced sugar'. Roll it up like a Swiss Roll to enclose the filling. Cut into slices about one inch thick and lay them, cut side down, on a greased baking tray. Allow to prove and bake at 220°C (425°F, Reg 7) for about 10 minutes and then a further 10-15 minutes at 200°C (400°F, Reg 6) or a little lower if necessary until evenly brown. An extra sprinkle of sugar just before baking gives a lovely glaze. Allow to cool for five minutes until set and then cool on a wire rack.

LARDY CAKES

Northern lardy cakes are made with currants and caraway seeds. Those from the South traditionally had no fruit but were flavoured with mixed sweet spices: cinnamon, nutmeg, ginger, cloves or mace.

Use about 1lb (450-500g) of prepared and risen dough, 2oz (50g) each of lard or vegetarian white fat, granulated sugar and currants plus one teaspoonful of caraway seeds. Roll out the dough and, as in the folded method, dab half the lard over two-thirds of the dough. Sprinkle with half the sugar, fold the plain third over and over again. Press the 'seams', turn the dough and repeat the rolling and spreading with lard and sugar. Add the currants and caraway seeds and fold again. Press gently into a greased shallow tin and mark deeply with diamond shaped cuts.

Allow to prove and then bake at 220°C (425°F, Reg 7) for 10 minutes and then at 200°C (400°F, Reg 6) for 25-35 minutes more. Leave in the tin for a few minutes for the sinful lard and sugar to be absorbed and then turn out, upside down, on a wire rack to cool. Lardy cakes are best eaten broken into pieces and slightly warm on a cold day, and not too often!

FRUIT LOAVES AND TEA BREADS

You can make fruit loaves and tea breads from plain yeast dough made with all wholemeal flour or half and half wholemeal and strong white bread flour. You should make the dough in the ordinary way and after the first rising proceed as follows. Try to keep the fat and sugar content low but don't skimp on the fruit, nuts, peel or savoury flavourings.

Use about 1lb (450g) of risen dough for each loaf, which can be baked in a 6" (15cm) square or round tin or a large loaf tin. Depending on your choice of additional ingredients there are two good ways of adding them to the basic dough. Tear up the risen dough into egg size pieces in a large bowl, add about 2oz (50g) of your chosen fat (vegetable margarine, oil, butter or lard) and 2oz (50g) of sweetening (soft brown or Demerara sugar or half and half sugar and honey or golden syrup) for sweet loaves. Squeeze strongly and work well together by hand or in a mixer at low speed for a minute until the mixture is smooth. Add flavourings. blend well and fill into the greased baking tin.

Alternatively, pat out the risen dough to about ½" (1cm) thick, spread with half the added ingredients and roll up loosely. Repeat this with the other half of the extras, then roll up again and place in the tin.

Add any toppings when the dough is in the tin and leave to rise in a warm place for a second time until about doubled in size. Bake at 200°C (400°F, Reg 6) for about 30 minutes.

Variations for sweet loaves
- fig and treacle:
  use black treacle as sweetener and 4oz (110g) chopped figs, raisins, sultanas, and peel or any dried fruit mixture.
- apricot and walnut:
  4oz (110g) chopped, dried apricots, 2oz (50g) broken walnuts.
- orange and raisin:
  the thinly peeled and chopped rind of two large oranges plus the juice of one and up to 4oz (110g) raisins.
- apple and sultanas:
  4oz (110g) each of cored and finely chopped apple and sultanas.

Sweet toppings

Sprinkle these onto the dough before the second rising.
- tablespoon of Demerara sugar plus half teaspoon of suitable ground spice such as cinnamon, ginger or mixed cake spice.
- sesame, poppy or sunflower seeds, finely chopped or milled nuts or stem ginger.
- crumbled Weetabix or crushed cornflakes stirred together with a scant tablespoon of oil and a little sugar.
- 'Streusel' or crumble topping made of 2oz (50g) flour with 1oz (25g) soft margarine and 1oz (25g) sugar rubbed in.

Variations for Savoury Loaves

These are good with soup or sliced and spread with cheese. Blend in the fat as for the sweet loaves but omit the sweetening, of course.
- nut breads:
  use 4-6oz (100-150g) of finely broken nuts (walnuts, cashew, peanuts or chestnuts in season) and 1-2 teaspoons of curry powder, ground cumin or coriander. Chopped mushrooms are good with this.
- onion and tomato:
  blend one tablespoon each of tomato purée and oil and use as part of the fat, one medium onion finely chopped.
- soup bread:
  blend into the enriched dough a packet of dried soup mix, mushroom, onion or oxtail are all good.

Savoury Toppings
- chopped or milled nuts with a little coarse salt and black pepper.
- crumbled Weetabix or cornflakes stirred with a scant tablespoon of oil plus a little celery salt, dried onion or garlic flakes.
- 'Streusel' topping (omitting the sugar) adding some finely grated cheese. Some of the flour may be replaced by oatmeal.
- Caraway, poppy and sesame seeds may be added.

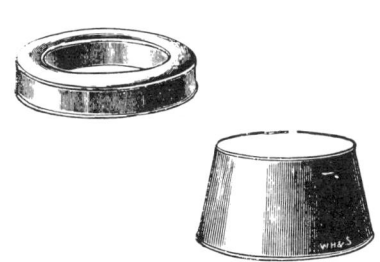

BAKING FOR THE FAMILY

Tips for Success with Pastry

Flour

If your family is not used to wholemeal pastry, you may find they accept it more readily if you mix half-and-half with your usual self-raising flour and gradually increase the proportion of wholemeal! Add a teaspoon of baking powder per 4oz (110g) of plain wholemeal flour. The techniques need slight modification to cater for the wheat germ and high fibre content of the flour, but your efforts will be rewarded with a satisfying and nutritious pastry, full of flavour.

Fats

These are better used at room temperature than refrigerator chilled, so that they may be rubbed into the flour lightly and easily. The soft 'dietary' margarines contain a very high proportion of water, which will upset the balance of the ingredients, so try to avoid their use in pastry. A combination of butter or margarine and solid vegetable fat gives good results and a little oil makes the pastry crisp and you won't need to use so much water. However, if you use too much oil the pastry will be unmanageably soft and crumbly.

Water

The water should be as cold as possible and sprinkled in sparingly; use just a little less than you think you need to start with – it is easier to add a few drops more than to try and manipulate or 'dry out' a too sticky dough. The pastry should just cling together to form a smooth ball; too much water will make the pastry tough and hard and it will shrink in the oven.

Resting

Try to plan your timetable to allow the pastry 15 minutes resting time before you roll it out. This helps the gluten content of the flour develop its elastic properties; keep it covered with cling film in a cool place and it will be much easier to manage. Don't stretch it to fit the baking tin – it will only shrink.

BASIC WHOLEMEAL SHORTCRUST PASTRY

8oz (225g) wholemeal flour
2 rounded teaspoons baking powder pinch of salt
4oz (110g) mixed fats
(half butter or margarine, half solid vegetable fat)
cold water to mix.

Sift the dry ingredients into a bowl. Cut the fats into the flour, then rub in with the fingertips as lightly as possible, lifting the mixture up well to aerate it. The mixture should look like bread crumbs. Mix with just enough very cold water to make a dough which clings together and leaves the bowl clean. Rest the dough for 15 minutes and then roll out as required. Bake at 200°C (400°F, Reg 6).

FILLED PASTRY PLAITS

Roll out the pastry to an oblong and spread the filling down the middle third. Slice the sides into strips about 1" (2-3cm) wide like a fringe, then fold the strips alternately over the filling.

Suggested sweet fillings are:
- fresh soft fruit in season
- sliced ripe pears or apple
- dried fruit, a mixture, or Christmas mincemeat
- dried apricots soaked and chopped with a little ground almonds. Use a little spiced sugar if it needs sweetening or sprinkle the top with a few chopped nuts or sesame seeds.

Savoury fillings might be:
- sliced mushrooms with tomato
- sausage meat or minced cooked meat with finely sliced onion and a little chutney or sauce to moisten
- blanched chopped spinach or broccoli with cottage or other cheese, bound with beaten egg
- roughly chopped mixed nuts, wholemeal crumbs and beaten egg, well seasoned, makes a tasty and satisfying vegetarian main course.

PLAIN WHOLEMEAL SCONES

8oz (225g) wholemeal flour
2 heaped teaspoons baking powder pinch of salt
2oz (50g) butter, margarine or a mixture
1 egg beaten with milk to make ¼ pint (150ml)

Preheat oven to 220°C (425°F, Reg 7). Sift the dry ingredients and rub in the fat. Reserve a little of the egg/milk mixture to glaze the scones then, working as quickly and lightly as possible, use a knife to mix the rest of the liquid into the dry ingredients to make a soft but not sticky dough (it needs to be much softer than for pastry). Turn out onto a floured board, draw all together into a smooth shape without deep cracks. Flip it upside down onto a greased and floured baking sheet and pat or roll into one large thick round. Brush with the reserved egg wash, cut right through with a sharp knife into triangles and bake straight away for about 15-20 minutes. Alternatively the mix may be stamped into rounds before baking and served split with jam and cream.

For variety add 2oz (50g) dried fruit and a tablespoon of Demerara sugar or a small grated unpeeled cooking apple with a pinch of cinnamon and a tablespoon of sugar. Savoury scones may be seasoned with a little dry mustard and a pinch of cayenne pepper, a little extra salt and grated, strong cheese or chopped salted peanuts. Sprinkle the tops with poppy or sesame seeds after brushing with egg wash or milk. You can also use it as a scone 'pizza' base with your choice of toppings.

AMERICAN CORNBREAD MUFFINS

One small onion, very finely chopped
one generous tablespoon cooking oil
3oz (75g) plain wholemeal flour
3oz (75g) maize meal
1½ teaspoons baking powder
½ teaspoon salt
one teaspoon Demerara sugar
one egg beaten and made up to just over ¼ pint (150ml) with milk
2oz grated cheese

These savoury buns are delicious as part of a vegetarian meal. They use baking powder as a raising agent and maize meal with wholemeal flour.

Preheat oven to 200°C (400°F, Reg 6). Gently fry the onion in the heated oil until it is soft. Sift and blend together all the dry ingredients and then add the onions and oil, egg and milk and cheese. Divide the mixture into eight or ten bun tins, well greased and bake for 10-12 minutes. They are best eaten warm.

ANADAMA BREAD

Anadama bread is also known as ash bread or hoe bread, indicating that the dough was dropped onto a hearthstone and cooked directly over an open fire. Most recipes for it use pre-cooked maize meal; in thrifty households the cook would have used left over breakfast corn pone (maize porridge) and baked the bread very quickly in a similar way to the oven bottom or stotty cake from the North of England.

½ pint (300ml) water
2oz (50g) maize meal
teaspoon salt
3oz (75g) margarine
4oz (110g) molasses or syrup
1oz (25g) fresh yeast
About ½ pint (275ml) water
1lb 4oz (½kg) strong wholemeal flour

Cook the first five ingredients together in a pan over moderate heat, stirring until thick and bubbly.

Leave until lukewarm and then make a stiff dough by adding the yeast (or its equivalent as dried yeast used according to the instructions on the packet) in the additional water and the flour. Knead to make the dough smooth and elastic and leave to rise until doubled in size. Knock it back, shape smoothly and place in a 2lb loaf tin. Brush the top with softened margarine and sprinkle with maize meal. Leave it to rise again until doubled in size and bake at 190°C (375°F, Reg 5) for 50-60 minutes. Cool on a rack. It is best not to cut the loaf until the next day.

CHOCOLATE SLAB CAKE

10oz (285g) wholemeal flour
3 rounded teaspoons baking powder
12oz (340g) soft brown sugar
8oz (225g) soft margarine or butter
4 rounded tablespoons cocoa
8 fl.oz (200ml) water
¼ pint (150ml) sour cream or thick plain yoghurt
½-1 teaspoon vanilla essence or ground cinnamon
2 large eggs, beaten

Preheat the oven to 190°C (375°F, Reg 5). Line a 12" x 8" x 2" (30cm x 20cm x 5cm) tin with greased greaseproof paper. Sift the flour and the baking powder into a large bowl. Put the sugar, fat, cocoa and water into a pan and gently bring to the boil, stirring well. Pour this over the flour and beat, add the sour cream or yoghurt, vanilla essence and beaten eggs. Mix thoroughly and scrape into the prepared tin. Bake for 35-40 minutes until a skewer comes out clean. When cooled to just warm pour the chocolate fudge frosting over it.

CHOCOLATE FUDGE FROSTING

4oz (110g) butter or margarine
3 tablespoons milk
2 tablespoons cocoa
8oz (225g) sifted icing sugar
chopped nuts up to 3oz (75g) if liked

Melt the margarine or butter in the warmed milk, beat in the cocoa and gently bring to the boil. Beat in the sugar and the nuts if you want them. Beating all the time, allow to cool for 3-4 minutes and then pour the mixture over the warm cake. If you prefer you can omit the nuts and use them to decorate the cake portions, along with cherries, silver dragees, crystallized ginger, etc.

FRUIT LOAF

9oz (250g) wholemeal flour
1 teaspoon mixed spice
1 teaspoon bicarbonate of soda
½ teaspoon salt
2oz (50g) sultanas
2oz (50g) raisins
1oz (25g) currants or peel
1 tablespoon cooking oil
2 tablespoons black treacle
about ¼ pint (150ml) milk
1oz (25g) brown sugar

Sift the dry ingredients and stir in the dried fruit. Warm together the milk, oil, treacle and sugar (a tablespoonful of plain malt extract may be substituted for one of black treacle). Stir this liquid into the dry mixture, adding a little extra milk if necessary to make a dropping mixture. Using a well greased loaf tin, fill the mixture well into the corners; bake at 170°C (325°F, Reg 3) for 45-60 minutes. Test with a skewer. Leave to set for a while and then cool on a wire rack. The loaf is best kept for two or three days before cutting.

The dried fruit in this recipe can be varied to suit your taste: chopped and stoned dates and walnuts are very good.

COCONUT BISCUITS

These biscuits are very easy for children to make. The quantities given make about 30 biscuits.
4oz (110g) wholemeal flour
4oz (110g) desiccated coconut
4oz (110g) soft margarine
4oz (110g) soft brown sugar
pinch of salt
1 egg

Put all the ingredients in a bowl and beat together to form a stiff dough. Add a little more flour if it is a bit sticky (it depends on the size of the egg). Roll into small balls, flatten onto greased baking sheets and bake at about 170°C (325°F, Reg 3) for 20-25 minutes. Cool on a wire rack and store in an airtight tin.

FESTIVE FARE

Here are some variations on traditional favourites, together with international specialities and a few ideas which younger members of the family may like to try.

BIRNBROT

This is a Pear Bread from Switzerland.

10oz (275g) wholemeal flour
2oz (50g) soft butter or margarine
1 egg, lightly beaten
5 fl.oz (150ml) warm milk
1 sachet Easy-blend yeast

Sift together the wholemeal flour with a generous pinch of salt and the sugar. Rub in the soft butter or margarine and stir in the sachet of dried yeast. Mix with the egg and warm milk and knead for about 10 minutes to make a springy elastic dough. Shape into a smooth ball, place in a greased bowl, cover with polythene and a clean cloth and leave in a warm place until it has doubled in size.

Meanwhile prepare the filling that, to be authentic, should be made from dried pears although fresh cooking pears may be used as long as the final purée is really thick. Alternatively concentrated fruit purée is obtainable from wholefood shops.

8oz (225g) dried pears
4oz (110g) stoned prunes
5-7 fl oz (150-200ml) water with the juice of a lemon
2-3 oz (50-75g) raisins
2 tablespoons sugar
grated rind of a lemon
½ teaspoon ground cinnamon
½ teaspoon ground nutmeg
a little kirsch liqueur or red wine

Coarsely chop the dried pears and the prunes and cook until soft in the water and lemon juice. Strain off any remaining liquid, then purée the fruit, add the raisins, sugar, lemon rind and spices together with a little kirsch liqueur or red wine, but take care not to make the purée runny.

When the dough is well risen, warm a large Swiss roll tin and spread with a tablespoon of soft butter. Punch the dough down well to knock out any large air bubbles, lay it on a floured 18" (45cm) square of waxed or greaseproof paper and roll it out to about ½" (1cm) thick. Spread the thick fruit purée smoothly to within one inch of three of the edges. Fold the two sides in about ½" (1cm) and roll up the dough from the fully spread end, using the paper to help you transfer it to the baking tin. Prick with a thin skewer, cover lightly with polythene and leave in a warm place until puffy.

Then bake for the first 10 minutes at 200°C (400°F, Reg 6). Reduce the temperature to 180°C (350°F, Reg 4) for a further 40-50 minutes and then cool on a wire tray. The finished loaf may be drizzled with thin lemon icing.

BUCHE DE NÖEL

Buche de Nöel is a chocolate and chestnut log from France. Fine crops of chestnuts are harvested in Central and Southern France and used in cooking and confectionery. Marrons glacés are a speciality made from chestnuts cooked and crystallised in heavy sugar syrup. You can buy tinned chestnut purée for this luxurious French Christmas treat; ensure that you have the unsweetened purée.

For the cake
2oz (50g) cocoa or carob powder (not drinking chocolate)
2oz (50g) wholemeal flour
1 teaspoon baking powder
pinch of salt
3 eggs
4oz (110g) caster sugar

For the filling
one can (15½oz) unsweetened chestnut purée
6oz (175g) fromage frais or whipped double cream
3oz (75g) soft brown sugar
1 tablespoon instant coffee dissolved in 1-2 tablespoons of chocolate or coffee liqueur (or water)

Grease and line a large Swiss roll type tin 13" x 9" (33 x 23cm) with greased greaseproof paper. Sieve the flour, baking powder, carob or cocoa powder and salt together twice. Put in a warm place whilst you whisk together the eggs and the caster sugar until very thick and pale and the whisk leaves a 'trail'. Carefully cut and fold in the flour mixture and pour into the prepared tin, filling well into the corners. Bake at 200°C (400°F, Reg 6) for about 12 minutes until it is well risen and the surface is springy when pressed. Do not overbake.

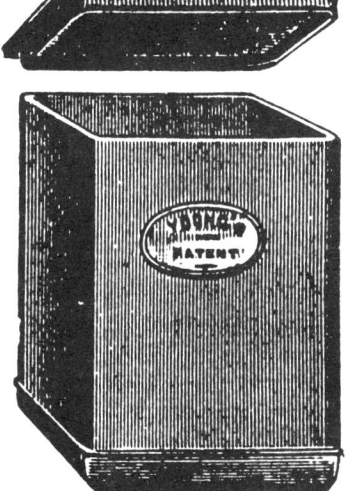

Hygienic Flour or Bread Bin.

Turn it upside down onto a clean cloth dusted with sugar or cornflour resting on a wire rack, peel off the paper, trim the crisp edges away and roll up the sponge with the cloth inside. Leave to cool completely.

Soften the chestnut purée and blend all the filling ingredients together thoroughly. Unroll the cooled cake, spread with about half the chestnut mixture and re-roll. Use the rest of the mixture to cover the outside of the cake; work with a fork to resemble bark and decorate to choice: chocolate curls, holly sprigs, marzipan mushrooms or simply a sprinkle of icing sugar 'snow'.

APFELSTRUDEL

Apfelstrudel originated in Hungary and is now associated with Austria. If you use wholemeal flour and breadcrumbs it will taste far better than the overpriced and over-sweetened shop versions. Strudel pastry is low in fat and versatile and may be used with both savoury and sweet fillings. The cooked pastries freeze well and may then be gently reheated after thawing. A little experience may be needed to stretch the dough out really thinly but your practice strudel will be tasty anyway, so keep trying! The quantities given will make a pastry for 4-6 people.

5oz (150g) wholemeal flour
pinch of salt
1 tablespoon of sunflower oil
about 4 fl.oz (100ml) warm water

Mix the flour, salt, oil and sufficient warm water to make a soft dough. Knead it vigorously by slapping it on a working surface until it is elastic (about 5-10 minutes). Brush the ball of dough with a little extra oil, cover with a warm bowl turned upside down and rest it for 15-20 minutes.

Meanwhile prepare the apple filling.

2oz (50g) wholemeal breadcrumbs
½oz (15g) butter or oil
3 or 4 crisp apples, cored and grated or finely chopped, no need to peel
3-4oz (75-100g) raisins
1-2oz (25-50g) flaked almonds
1 teaspoon ground cinnamon
grated rind of a lemon
1-2 teaspoons runny honey or maple syrup

Lightly fry the breadcrumbs in the butter or oil and then mix well together with the other ingredients. Spread a cloth on your working surface and sprinkle with flour. Start by rolling out the dough but then use your hands underneath to stretch and pull the dough until it is as thin as possible – you should be able to see any pattern on the cloth. Try not to tear holes but if they occur, don't worry.

When your patience is as thin as the pastry you can sprinkle the filling evenly over the dough, brush the edges with oil and roll up the strudel by lifting one end of the cloth; coil it onto a greased baking sheet, brush with oil and bake at 200°C (400°F, Reg 6) for 40-50 minutes. Brush the top whilst hot with a little honey or maple syrup or leave until cold and then sift with icing sugar or drizzle with thin lemon flavoured icing.

YULETIDE GARLANDS

For the children to bake as an edible gift or to decorate the Christmas tree (the garlands will soften in a room atmosphere – but perhaps they won't hang there long enough for that to occur!) The quantities given will make between eight and sixteen depending on the size.

5oz (150g) butter
8oz (225g) wholemeal flour
3oz (75g) soft brown sugar
grated rind of a lemon
1 beaten egg

Rub the butter into the flour until it looks like fine breadcrumbs. Add the sugar and rind and mix with enough egg to make a soft pliable dough. Knead until free of cracks and divide into marble size balls (it will make perhaps a hundred of them). Arrange them firmly touching in circles on greased baking sheets, from six to twelve in each circle, and bake at 190°C (375°F, Reg 5) for 15-20 minutes until golden. Leave to set for five minutes and then carefully remove to finish cooling on a wire rack. Store in an airtight tin for up to two weeks or freeze for up to two months. Use ribbon or tinsel and holly sprigs to hang from the Christmas tree or to decorate a party table.

FLORENTINES

A real luxury, horrendously expensive from the confectioners but easy to make, florentines would be an acceptable gift if packed in a pretty box or a wide necked jar.

2oz (50g) butter
2oz (50g) Demerara sugar
1 tablespoon golden syrup
2oz (50g) sifted wholemeal flour
1½-2oz (35-50g) each of cherries, walnuts, mixed peel and blanched almonds, all finely chopped
a few flaked almonds to decorate

Melt together the butter, sugar and syrup. Add the sifted flour and the fruit, nuts and peel. Drop generous teaspoonfuls well apart on greased baking sheets and put two or three flakes of almonds on each. Bake at 170°C (325°F, Reg 3) for 10-15 minutes. Whilst they are still warm neaten the shapes into circles by drawing the 'frayed' edges together with a fork. Lift off when set and cool before storing in an airtight tin. Melted chocolate may be spread on the backs to make them even more luxurious.

SAVOURY ROULADE

This is an impressive dish for a buffet or supper party, the choice of filling to complete it depending on the inspiration from your store cupboard; use curd or cottage cheese as a filling base to keep the fat content down, but you may like to add some full fat cream cheese or whipped double cream for a special treat. The filling needs to be firm but spreadable, well flavoured and carefully seasoned.

Here are some suggestions:
- plain curd or drained cottage cheese beaten until smooth with chopped chives or other fresh herbs stirred in and seasoned, then add your selected addition:
- finely flaked smoked fish with a little tartare sauce
- chopped cooked ham or poultry trimmings with mixed mustard or chutney
- shrimps or tuna fish with tomato purée or mayonnaise
- pesto (an intensely flavoured basil sauce from Italy)
- chopped olives, anchovies, gherkins, capers or pickled walnuts
- fine shreds of strongly flavoured continental sausage
- finely chopped or ground roasted or fresh nuts of all kinds
- a little crumbled hearty blue cheese (Mycella or Roquefort are good)
- a pinch of 'hot' spice (chilli, cayenne or curry powder) with cooked, drained and crushed red beans.

BASIC ROULADE

To serve six:
1 medium onion, peeled and finely chopped
8oz (225g) fresh spinach (frozen may be substituted – cook lightly)
1oz (25g) butter or margarine

2 tablespoons chopped parsley
salt, pepper, ground nutmeg
4 eggs
2oz (50g) wholemeal flour
8oz (225g) curd or cottage cheese as base for the filling

Grease and line a shallow tin about 8" x 12" (20cm x 30cm) with greased greaseproof paper. Wash and drain the spinach well, discarding only the coarsest stems. Heat the butter or margarine in a saucepan and sauté the onion for a minute without browning it. Then add the spinach, turning and cooking it over a high heat until all the water has evaporated and the leaves are well wilted, though not pulpy.

Remove from the heat, stir in the parsley and seasoning and then chop up well (but don't purée or process it). Whilst it cools whisk the eggs with a pinch of salt in a large bowl until the whisk leaves a trail. Carefully fold in the spinach and the flour and pour into the prepared tin. Bake at 200°C (400°F, Reg 6) for 10-12 minutes until it is even and firm to the touch – but do not over bake it.

When cooked turn it upside down onto a fresh piece of greaseproof paper, remove the cooking paper and roll up the roulade with the clean paper inside. Cool on a rack. It may then be unrolled, spread with the filling and rolled up again, ready to serve.

CHRISTMAS CAKE

Wholemeal flour is excellent for baking cakes. This fine old recipe makes a traditional Christmas cake which is rich and moist yet not too heavy.

8oz (225g) wholemeal flour
8oz (225g) soft brown sugar
4 eggs
8oz (225g) butter or margarine
½ teaspoon of salt
4 tablespoons of brandy
1 tablespoon of treacle
2oz (50g) chopped almonds or walnuts
grated rind of one lemon and one orange
8oz (225g) raisins
2oz (50g) mixed candied peel
12oz (350g) currants
8oz (225g) sultanas
2oz (50g) glacé cherries
½ teaspoon fresh grated nutmeg
½ teaspoon mixed spice

Before making the cake soak the fruit in the brandy overnight. Grease an 8" (20cm) round cake tin with greaseproof paper. Set the oven to 140°C (275°F, Reg 1).

Sieve the flour, spices and salt into a bowl. Beat the butter and sugar together in another bowl until they become light and fluffy. Then beat the eggs into the creamed butter and sugar a tablespoonful at a time. Fold the flour and spices gently into this mixture. Stir in the treacle, fruit, peel and grated rind. Spoon the mixture into the tin and cover with two layers of greaseproof paper with a 2" (5cm) diameter hole cut in the top.

Bake on the lower shelf of the oven for 4½ hours and then test to see if the cake is cooked by pushing a steel knitting needle or a skewer into the cake. If it comes out clean the cake is cooked. If uncooked mixture clings to the skewer bake for a further fifteen minutes and test again. When the cake is cold turn it out of the tin and wrap in greaseproof paper before storing in an airtight tin. For a really succulent cake poke some holes in the top and let three or four tablespoons of brandy soak in.

CHRISTMAS PLUM PUDDING

Curiously, plum puddings don't contain plums! But they do have a glorious mixture of fruit, spices and wholemeal flour which, when boiled or steamed as a good pudding should be, goes wonderfully with brandy butter, cream or yoghurt. In the past huge, rich heavy puddings served to eke out the Christmas goose. This recipe gives an altogether lighter pudding. It will make one large or two smaller puddings – one for Christmas and one, perhaps, for the freezer!

5oz (125g) wholemeal flour
2oz (50g) chopped peel
5oz (125g) brown breadcrumbs
4oz (110g) moist brown sugar
4oz (110g) vegetable suet
2oz (50g) grated carrot
4oz (110g) currants
4oz (110g) raisins
juice and grated rind of a lemon
1 teaspoon baking powder
½ teaspoon fresh grated nutmeg
1 pint (600ml) milk
1 teaspoon mixed spice
pinch of salt

Soak the fruit and breadcrumbs in the milk for at least an hour. Stir in all the other ingredients and mix well. Turn the mixture into one large or two small pudding basins. Cover the top of each bowl with a double layer of greased greaseproof paper. Cover with tied down baking foil or a tied down pudding cloth. Place the bowl in a large saucepan and fill with water until it is halfway up the side of the bowl. Cover with a tight fitting lid and gently boil the pudding for a total of six hours.

If you are making the puddings in advance boil them for about four hours and then for another two on Christmas Day. The puddings can be cooked in a pressure cooker for a shorter cooking time; the instruction book should tell you what is required. You might even be able to do it in a microwave oven but a magnificent old recipe such as this deserves to be boiled in a pudding cloth.

USE YOUR OATS

Do you remember being urged to 'eat up your porridge because it is good for you'? Maybe our mothers were wiser than they realised because recent research in nutrition has shown that the risk of coronary heart disease and diabetes may be reduced if oats are part of our diet! As well as these valuable properties, oats are full of flavour and give a welcome boost to the texture and nutritive content of many 'family favourite' recipes. Try substituting oatmeal for about a quarter of the flour in your usual crumble toppings for puddings or add a little to pastry, especially for savoury dishes.

Oatmeal may be used instead of bread crumbs for many recipes. Try using it to coat fish before cooking under a moderate grill or in a non-stick frying pan to give a good textured finish to meat, fish or vegetarian 'burgers.' A tasty stuffing to use with fish or chicken might consist of oatmeal, finely grated onion well seasoned with herbs and moistened with stock or beaten egg. Try it as a thickener for home-made soups – especially good with onions or leeks.

Biscuits containing oatmeal scorch easily if cooked at a too high a temperature. A more moderate oven heat will result in lightly coloured, crisp biscuits provided that the cooking time is extended a little.

PROPER PORRIDGE

Add one measure of oatmeal to three or four measures of cold water, add salt to taste and bring to a gentle boil over a moderate heat, stirring all the while to prevent lumps. Turn off the heat, cover the pan and leave to stand for a few minutes to finish cooking. Stir well and serve in warm bowls with milk and sugar. Porridge also cooks well in a microwave oven.

SODA BREAD

These quickly made breads need not be made from strong (high gluten content) flours. Indeed the inclusion of oatmeal will give a softer, cake-like texture which is typical of these loaves and scones. Eat them with soup, salad, paté or cheese; well flavoured jams also complement them. It is best to eat them whilst they are still warm as they stale quickly.

4oz (110g) oatmeal
4oz (110g) wholemeal flour
½ teaspoon salt
2 rounded teaspoons baking powder

¼ pint (150ml) buttermilk (or fresh milk soured with lemon juice, or half-and-half milk stirred with plain yoghurt)

Preheat the oven to 220°C (450°F, Reg 7-8). Sift all the dry ingredients twice but put all the coarse particles left in the sieve back into the mixing bowl. Then mix with the liquid to make a soft dough; it should be almost sticky. Quickly pat into a thick round, place on a greased and floured baking sheet, cut into sections and bake straight away for about 20 minutes. Cool on a rack.

SCOTTISH OATCAKES
4 tablespoons medium oatmeal
1 teaspoon salt
a little oil or lard
warm water to mix

Mix the oatmeal and salt and rub in the lard if you use it or stir in the oil. Mix with enough warm water to make a soft dough which just clings together. Roll out straight away on a board dusted with extra oatmeal and cut into shapes with a plain cutter. You may need to add a little more water to the trimmings to be able to roll them out again. Bake at 170°C (325°F, Reg 3) for 20-25 minutes until they are crisp but not brown.

STAFFORDSHIRE OATCAKES
These are really soft pancakes, full of holes, that can be eaten with jam or honey or spread with a savoury filling, rolled up and topped with cheese or herb sauce.

4oz (110g) oatmeal
4oz (110g) wholemeal flour
1 teaspoon fresh yeast (or your choice of dried yeast)
1 teaspoon sugar
1 teaspoon salt
¾ pint (400ml) warm milk and water

Stir the fresh yeast into a little of the liquid, with the sugar and add the rest of the liquid. Stir this into the dry ingredients to make a smooth batter. If you are using dried yeast follow the instructions on the packet. Leave the batter, covered with a plate, in a warm place to become frothy. Heat a heavy frying pan over a moderate heat, oil it lightly, stir the batter well and fry a small teacupful at a time, flipping the pancake over to lightly brown the second side. This will make six to

eight pancakes. The batter can be stored in the refrigerator and used on another day.

SAVOURY SNAPS

These are flavoured with cheese and seasonings; sesame seeds and oatmeal add interesting texture.

4oz (110g) wholemeal flour
2oz (50g) oatmeal
one flat teaspoon salt (celery, onion or garlic salt are good if you have them)
pinch of cayenne pepper
½ teaspoon dry mustard powder
2oz (50g) margarine
2oz (50g) grated strong cheese
two tablespoons sesame seeds
one egg yolk and a little milk, or just milk alone

Sift the dry ingredients, rub in the margarine, add the cheese and sesame seeds and then mix with the egg and milk to a stiffish dough. Roll out to about ½" (1cm) thick, sprinkle extra sesame seeds on the surface and gently roll again to press them into the dough. Cut into triangles or fingers and bake at 190°C (375°F, Reg 5) for about 15-20 minutes. Cool completely before storing in an airtight tin.

'DIGESTIVE' BISCUITS

Digestive biscuits are well worth making at home and you may adjust the amount of sugar to taste.

4oz (110g) wholemeal flour
4oz (110g) oatmeal
½ teaspoon bicarbonate of soda
3oz (75g) soft margarine
1oz (25g) soft brown sugar
1 egg yolk
a little milk

Sieve the dry ingredients, rub in the margarine, add the sugar and mix with the egg yolk and a little milk to a not-too-firm dough. Roll out to about the thickness of a one pound coin, cut into shapes and bake at 180°C (350°F, Reg 4) for about 12-15 minutes. Cool thoroughly before storing in an airtight tin.

OATMEAL & RAISIN BISCUITS

3oz (75g) just melted butter or margarine

5oz (150g) soft brown sugar
7oz (200g) oatmeal
3oz (75g) wholemeal flour
½ teaspoon bicarbonate of soda
3oz (75g) raisins
1 beaten egg
a little milk if necessary

Mix the butter or margarine, sugar and raisins, add sifted dry ingredients and the egg plus a little milk to bind the mixture. Roll into balls (it will make about two dozen) and flatten slightly on greased baking sheets, allowing room for them to spread. Bake at 180°C (350°F, Reg 4) for about 12-15 minutes.

greased baking sheets and flatten with a wet fork. Bake at 190°C (375°F, Reg 5) for 15-18 minutes. Loosen from the tins when you remove them from the oven, but leave to set before completely cooling on a wire rack and storing in an airtight tin.

CHOCOLATE OATMEAL BISCUITS

4oz (110g) soft margarine
3oz (75g) soft brown sugar
½-1 teaspoon vanilla essence
less than one beaten egg
1½ tablespoons cocoa or carob powder
4oz (110g) wholemeal flour
2oz (50g) oatmeal
½ teaspoon baking powder

The quantities given make about two dozen biscuits. Cream the margarine and the sugar together and then beat in the vanilla essence and the beaten egg. Sift the cocoa or carob powder, flour, oatmeal and baking powder and add to the creamed mixture. Place heaped teaspoons on

APRICOT SQUARES

These may be served as a sweet course or as a cake and other dried fruit may be substituted for the apricot.

4oz (110g) dried apricots
6-7fl.oz (200ml) of water
1 tablespoon sugar
2 teaspoons of cornflour
8oz (225g) oatmeal
4oz (110g) wholemeal flour
1 level teaspoon baking powder
4oz (110g) soft margarine
4oz (110g) soft brown sugar
less than ¼ pint (150ml) milk
2 tablespoons Demerara sugar

If necessary soak the apricots and cook them with one tablespoon of sugar in the water and thicken with the cornflour. Blend together the oatmeal, flour and baking powder. Rub in the margarine, add the soft brown sugar and sufficient milk to mix to a scone-like dough. Roll out half of the dough and line a Swiss roll type of tine about 11" by 7" (28cm x 18cm). Spread the fruit filling over and cover with the other half of the dough. Brush the top with milk, sprinkle with the remaining sugar and prick the top with a fork. Bake at 180°C (350°F, Reg 4) for about 35 minutes, Mark into pieces whilst still warm but leave to cool before removing from the tin.

YEASTED FRUIT LOAF

This unusual recipe produces a light, spongy cake but uses no eggs and very little sugar.

5oz (150g) wholemeal flour
3oz (75g) oatmeal
2 teaspoons mixed spice
1 teaspoon ground cinnamon
½ teaspoon salt
1oz (25g) soft margarine
1oz (25g) soft brown or Demerara sugar
3oz (75g) each of sultanas, raisins, chopped peel, chopped apple, chopped nuts (walnuts, cashews, brazils or a mixture)
½oz (about 10g) fresh yeast or the equivalent of dried yeast
6-8fl.oz (about 200ml) warm milk and water

If using fresh or granulated yeast activate it with a pinch of sugar and some of the warm yeast liquid. 'Easy-blend' should be mixed dry with the flour. Sieve the flour, spices, salt and oatmeal. rub in the margarine, add the sugar, fruit and nuts and stir together with all the warm liquid to make a dropping mixture, adding a little more milk if necessary. Divide the mixture between two small loaf tins which have been greased and floured. Leave in a warm place covered with a polythene bag until the mixture has risen and looks 'puffy'. Bake at 220°C (450°F, Reg 7) for about 10 minutes and then lower heat to 190°C (375°F, Reg 5) for a further 25-30 minutes. Test with a skewer, which should come out clean.

After cooling this loaf may be iced with thin lemon icing or before baking may be sprinkled with poppy or sesame seeds and a little granulated sugar.

CRANACAN

This is a delectable sweet originating in Scotland and made with the

The Empress Patent Cake Tins.

superb Scottish raspberries, but a mixture of soft fruits can be used, either fresh or just-thawed frozen ones. Lower caloried alternatives to cream might be plain yoghurt, smatana, creme fraiche or fromage frais. Apples, plums or rhubarb may be used in the place of raspberries, but of course need to be cooked lightly first and used when cold. This recipe serves four.

4 tablespoons oatmeal
8-12oz (250-350g) soft fruit
runny honey or caster sugar to taste
¼ pint each single & double cream

Toast the oatmeal on a flat baking sheet under a moderate grill until lightly and evenly browned, stirring it frequently so that it doesn't scorch, then leave it to cool. Drizzle the fruit with honey or sugar. Whip the creams until 'floppy' and sweeten lightly to taste. Just before serving spread the oatmeal, fruit and cream in layers in individual dishes so that the oatmeal stays crisp.

PARKINS & GINGERBREADS

These usually have a high ratio of sugar, syrup and treacle compared to the fat used and the raising agent is often bicarbonate of soda, the reaction of the one with the other creating the aeration necessary to raise the mixture. It is a good idea to get the cakes into the oven as soon as possible after mixing. Have the tin greased and lined and the oven pre-heating: baking temperatures need to be moderate or the cakes will caramelise too early, with the risk of being cracked, dry and, what's more, burned! They benefit from being kept for a few days before being cut, to allow the texture to soften or 'come again'. If you like a moist, sticky cake be resigned to using a recipe which contains a lot of syrup and don't overbake it.

The flavourings may be adjusted to your personal taste and some old recipes suggest a wide variety of ground spices including cinnamon, nutmeg, aniseed, cloves, cardamom, orange and lemon oils and vanilla as well as ginger. Even cayenne pepper and black pepper are mentioned, but this latter would have been Jamaica pepper – we know it as allspice. These warm and fragrant flavours would enable the cook to disguise the use of home produced fats like lard or clean clarified dripping as the shortening. Margarine, butter or vegetable oils are used now.

Medieval gingerbreads used honey as the sweetening and one early 15th century recipe suggests 'a quart of honey, warmed and skimmed, flavour with ginger, cinnamon and black pepper, raspings (i.e. breadcrumbs) to be added until it will take no more.

Shape and trim'. These rather brief instructions assumed that the cook knew very well how to finish it off; the mixture could be pressed into elaborately shaped wooden moulds or rolled flat and stamped out with cutters. After baking the cook would put the 'gilt on the gingerbread' – box leaves or cloves would be covered with gold leaf and stuck onto the shapes with egg white or sugar syrup. Favourite patterns were often of heraldic origin; shields, feathers, birds, portcullis and mythological animals. Sometimes they were mounted on canes to be carried as favours at jousting contests and were sold as 'fairings' to be taken home as presents for sweethearts and children from the large markets held on Feasts and Quarter Days.

SKIPTON PARKIN

This is an old recipe which was used by some ladies in Skipton to raise money for a Special Needs school. It was given to us when one of them visited Green's Mill.

8oz (225g) oatmeal
8oz (225g) wholemeal flour
1oz (25g) ground ginger
1 teaspoon bicarbonate of soda
½ teaspoon salt
4oz (110g) Demerara sugar
1lb (450g) golden syrup
4oz (110g) margarine
¼ pint (150ml) milk
2 beaten eggs

Sift the first five dry ingredients really well and add the sugar. Warm the syrup, milk and margarine and stir into the dry ingredients along with the beaten eggs. Using a greased and lined tin about 7" (18cm) square bake at 150°C (300°F, Reg 2-3) for about one and a half hours – but don't open the oven door for the first hour. Test with the clean skewer to check whether the cake is cooked. When it is done, leave it in the tin for a few minutes as these cakes are very 'tender' whilst still hot, then turn out onto a wire rack to finish cooling.

GINGER PARKIN

4oz (110g) golden syrup
4oz (110g) black treacle
3oz (75g) margarine or white vegetable fat
4oz (110g) wholemeal flour
1 teaspoon baking powder
½ teaspoon salt
2 heaped teaspoons ground ginger
8oz (225g) oatmeal
2oz (50g) soft brown sugar
1 teaspoon bicarbonate of soda
about 4fl.oz (120ml) milk

Line a 9" by 6" tin with greased paper. Warm together the syrup, treacle and fat. Sift the flour, baking powder, salt and ginger together, add oatmeal and sugar, mix well and make a hollow in the centre. Dissolve the bicarbonate of soda in the milk, pour into the warm syrup mixture and then all of the liquid ingredients into the dry. Mix very thoroughly, pour into prepared tin and bake at 165°C (325°F, Reg 3) for about 1½-2 hours. The parkin is best if kept in an airtight tin for a few days before cutting.

GINGERBREAD FOR CUT-OUT SHAPES OR MODELLING

10oz (275g) wholemeal flour
2 rounded teaspoons baking powder
1-1½ tablespoons ground ginger
1-1½ teaspoons ground cinnamon
3oz (75g) butter
4oz (110g) caster sugar
2 good tablespoons golden syrup
1 tablespoon treacle warmed enough to be runny, but not hot
1 beaten egg

Sieve the dry ingredients and rub in the butter. Add the sugar, syrup, treacle and beaten egg then mix and knead well to make a smooth crack-free dough; a few drops of milk may be needed. Rest the mixture for 15 minutes in a cool place, wrapped in cling film. Roll out the dough on a floured surface and cut into shapes with cutters or, for your own unique designs, use cardboard shapes to cut round with a sharp knife. Surface detail can be added by modelling with a cocktail stick or adding tiny pieces of dough for hair, eyes and so on. If you make traditional shapes to put on a Christmas Tree don't forget to make a hole for the hanging ribbon. Bake at 170°C (350°F, Reg 4) for 20-25 minutes. The dough will keep in the fridge if you don't want to use it all at once.

ROLY POLY, PUDDING & PIE

If you enjoy the occasional treat of a steamed pudding or raised savoury pie, you may prefer not to use the traditional suet or lard but replace them with vegetarian ingredients. Many food shops sell a 'suet' made from oils in the form of flakes or granules and a similar 'lard'. They are used in the same way as the original fats and the results are just as good.

'ROLY POLY'
(Suet Crust)

Use a tablespoon as a measure and allow the following amounts for each person:
2 rounded tablespoons wholemeal flour
pinch of salt
1 level teaspoon baking powder
1 rounded tablespoon suet
cold water to mix
savoury or sweet filling to choice

Blend all the dry ingredients really well, incorporating the suet last. Mix to a soft but not sticky dough with the cold water. Roll out to an oblong on a floured surface, not too thinly, and spread with the chosen filling to within an inch of the edges. Moisten the edges lightly and roll up gently, pinching the join and ends to seal. Wrap in greased foil and, allowing room to rise, fold and join the ends of the parcel. have a steamer ready over a pan of boiling water and cook the pudding for 1½-2 hours depending on the size and on the choice of the filling.

With a microwave oven you can cook a steamed pudding in 5-7 minutes. Use cooking parchment or greaseproof paper instead of foil and puncture the parcel to release the steam, following the directions for your own cooker.

Savoury Fillings
- minced meat with onions
- chopped ham or bacon with leeks and grated carrots
- chicken with chopped mushrooms or sweetcorn

Season well, moisten with a little stock or sauce

Sweet Roly Poly
- jam or syrup
- sweet mincemeat

- soft fruit, sliced rhubarb or apples, gooseberries, stoned plums, sweetened to taste

'PUDDING'
(Quick Crumble)

This makes a quick, tasty and nutritious topping for a fruit crumble. No weighing or rubbing-in is necessary, just multiply the quantity given by the number of servings you need. For each person allow:

1 rounded tablespoon wholemeal flour
1 rounded tablespoon oatmeal
1 level tablespoon Demerara or soft brown sugar
pinch of salt
1 tablespoon vegetable oil

Mix the dry ingredients in a bowl with a fork, crushing out any lumps in the sugar. Stir in the oil ensuring all is well blended. Use in the same way as a margarine based crumble mix; don't press it down too firmly over the fruit.

The mix also serves very well as a 'streusal' topping; use a scone or sweet yeast dough as a base in a sandwich tin, brush with oil, sprinkle with sugar and layer with halved, stoned plums or sliced apples. Flavour and sweeten to taste and top with a covering of the 'Quick Crumble'. A little ground almonds in the mixture is a delicious addition if you are using plums or apricots. Bake at 220°C (425°F, Reg 6-7) for about 20 minutes until the base is risen and brown and the fruit cooked.

'AND PIE'
(Hot Water Crust)

The art of hand-raising pies has almost died out, but you will find it easy to use Hot Water Crust to line a deep flan or spring form tin or oblong cake tin. Such a pie makes an impressive centre piece for a buffet, especially if you decorate the top with leaves, flowers and tassels cut from the pastry trimmings. This embellishment was reserved for savoury pies only – perhaps it saved the embarrassment of the pie being cut at the dining table for a main course and found to be filled with apple or rhubarb.

The pastry has a lower fat content than short-crust and is firmer when baked and so is good for picnic or packed lunch pies. Prepare the chosen filling in advance, not making it too moist; preheat the oven and

Old English Pudding Basin.

have a greased tin ready as the pastry is best used whilst it is still warm. The quantities given will make a pie to serve 4-6 people using a 6-7" tin (13-15cm) and filling with about 1lb 4oz (550g) of prepared meat. The oven setting for the first 20 minutes is 220°C (425°F, Reg 6-7).

12oz (350g) wholemeal flour
½ teaspoon salt
4oz (110g) solid vegetable fat or lard
just less than ¼ pint (140ml) water
beaten egg with a pinch of salt to glaze

Mix the flour and salt in a large bowl, melt the fat in the water in a saucepan and bring to the boil. Pour it all at once over the flour and blend quickly with a knife or wooden spoon. As soon as you can handle it, draw the dough together, knead lightly into a smooth ball, adding a little more water if it is a bit dry. Divide it roughly into two thirds and one third and keep the smaller piece for the lid warm and moist and wrapped in polythene. Use the larger piece to line the tin.

Working as quickly as you can press the dough out with a rolling pin but then use your fingers and make the lining fairly thin. Pack your chosen filling into the tin, leaving no air spaces. Roll the pastry lid to fit, damp and pinch the edges together well to join, trimming off any excess and re-rolling for the decorations. Prick the lid, make a good hole in the centre to release the steam and to allow you to test with a skewer for 'done-ness'. Brush the top well with beaten egg, place the tin on a baking sheet and into a preheated oven.

Bake at the given setting of 220°C (425°F, Reg 6-7) for the first 20-25 minutes and then reduce to 190°C (375°F, Reg 5) for a further 45-60 minutes. Cooking time will depend on the proportions of your tin and the choice of filling, meat fillings needing the longer cooking time. Cover the top with paper if it is browning too quickly. Allow to cool in the tin for at least ten minutes before turning out.

Fillings
- boned and skinned spare rib or lean belly pork cut into small pieces, seasoned with salt and pepper, sage and grated onion
- chicken and ham with mushrooms, grated nutmeg and herbs
- **vegetarian:**
  mixed, lightly cooked vegetables (leeks, carrots, cauliflower, onion, cooked pulses) with cheese, ground nuts or chestnut purée

Mix well before packing in the filling, season and use a little tomato or garlic purée or white sauce to moisten.

BAKING FOR SPECIAL OCCASIONS

Many countries use yeast in baking for festive occasions; the light texture of a dough enriched with butter and eggs and raised by yeast is unlike any other confectionery. It freezes well should you not wish to use it all at once; reheat it in a moderate oven for a short time and it will taste as fresh as newly baked.

Perhaps cake making started as a fanciful sideline of bread making. Baking powders, developed in America, were not available until the 1850s, so neither were self-raising flours. We may imagine a mother, making a treat for her family, using a portion of risen bread dough and adding a little sugar or honey, fruit and spice or caraway seeds. Richness and flavour were improved if she spared a scrap of freshly churned butter or even home rendered lard or dripping.

TIPS ON MAKING YEAST ENRICHED DOUGH

Fresh or granulated yeast needs to be activated in some of the liquid in the recipe before starting to make the dough. You add 'Easy-blend' dried yeast dry to the flour and then you can start to mix straight away. These two types of dried yeast will fail miserably if you confuse one with the other so read the instructions! You need about half the weight of dried yeast compared to fresh in a recipe. Activity of all the yeasts is retarded by extra fat and sugar in fancy doughs, so be prepared for rise and proof times to be longer. Rich yeast doughs are better if risen at lower fermentation temperatures (room temp. 15°C, 60°F)

BASIC BUN DOUGH

This dough may be adapted to produce a variety of sweet and savoury treats.

1lb (450g) plain wholemeal flour
½ teaspoon salt
1oz (25g) fresh yeast or a sachet of dried yeast
just less than ½ pint (275ml) warm water and milk
2oz (50g) sugar
3oz (75g) butter
1 beaten egg

Use about a quarter of the flour with the salt, yeast, a pinch of sugar and all the liquid to make a 'starter' batter, without lumps and leave it in a warm place to become frothy. Meanwhile mix the balance of the flour with the sugar and rub in the butter. When the batter is bubbly pour it into the dry mixture, add the beaten egg and mix to a smooth dough. Knead for a few minutes, adding a little more flour if it is very sticky. The dough should be softer than for bread.

Grease the clean bowl with a little oil or butter, roll the dough around in it, cover with polythene and a thick cloth and allow the dough to rise in a warm place until it has doubled in size. This bun dough is the basis of the following recipes from around the world.

TIN MOULDS.

England:
HOT CROSS BUNS
basic bun dough ingredients plus:
1 level teaspoon of each of ground cinnamon, mixed spice and ground nutmeg
3oz (75g) raisins
2oz (50g) chopped candied peel
almond paste or scraps of shortcrust pastry to make the cross on the tops 
egg/milk wash for tops
bun wash to glaze (made by heating gently together 2 tablespoons sugar with 2-3 tablespoons water until dissolved and syrupy)

Add the spices to the flour, sifting to eliminate lumps, at the beginning of the basic dough recipe. When the dough has risen knock it down, gently knead in the raisins and peel and then cut the dough into 18 pieces. Shape the pieces into round buns, place on greased baking sheets, brush with the egg wash and trim with the cross markers or cut a cross with a very sharp blade. Leave to prove in a warm place (15-30 minutes).

Bake at 230°C (450°F, Reg 8) for 10-15 minutes. When the buns are cooked brush the tops with the syrupy bun wash for a shiny finish.

England:
BATH BUNS
basic bun dough plus:
4oz (110g) sultanas
2oz (50g) chopped candied peel
egg/milk wash for the tops
a few roughly crushed sugar lumps or large coffee sugar crystals
bun wash (see above recipe)

Knock down the risen bun dough, gently knead in the sultanas and peel and cut the dough into 18 pieces. Shape into round buns, flattening the tops slightly. Place on greased baking sheets, brush with the egg wash and sprinkle the tops with the crushed sugar lumps or crystals. Prove for 15-30 minutes and bake at 230°C (450°F, Reg 8) for 10-15 minutes. As soon as they are cooked brush with the bun wash, being careful not to disturb the topping. Originally Bath Buns were decorated with 'comfits', aromatic seeds such as caraway or aniseed repeatedly dipped into boiling sugar until thickly coated.

Russia:
KHACHAPURI

This is a large soft bun-shaped loaf encasing a savoury or sweet filling. Cut into generous wedges, the savoury version is a scrumptious accompaniment to a soup or salad meal. You can serve the sweet one plain or with yoghurt or ice cream.

Make up a batch of the basic bun dough but use only 1oz (25g) sugar and 2oz (50g) of butter that should be just melted and added to the dough when the two portions are mixed together. Now you can either rise the dough first or proceed as follows with these additional ingredients:

6oz (175g) curd cheese
1 beaten egg
seasoning or flavourings e.g. for a savoury loaf fresh herbs, tomato puree, onion or garlic; for a sweet one dried fruit, sugar and spice, apple or other fruit.

Mix the egg with the cheese and add the flavouring. Shape the dough into a ball, punch down centre and put the cheese mixture into this hollow. Reshape the ball, pinching the edges to seal around the filling. Place on a greased baking sheet and cover with plastic to prevent it drying out whilst it proves to double its size.

Bake at 200°C, (400°F, Reg 6) for 35-40 minutes. As soon as it is baked brush with a salt wash (½ teaspoon of salt in a tablespoon of water) for a savoury kachapuri or the bun wash if it is sweet.

Czechoslovakia:
BUCHTY

These are small rich buns with a sweet filling:
- very thick plum or apricot jam
- cottage or curd cheese with
- raisins or chopped peel and sugar
- poppy seeds, half as much sugar as seeds, a little soft butter and some vanilla essence. This is a favourite in the Slavonic regions.

Make up a batch of the basic bun

dough but use only 12oz (350g) flour, 2oz (50g) butter and about ¼ pint (150ml) milk instead of ½ pint. Knock down the risen dough, divide into 10 or 12 equal portions and flatten them with a rolling pin. Add a portion of one of the fillings above. Pinch the edges together, prove the buns on greased baking sheets, brush with egg wash and make snips through the tops with scissors to allow the filling to show.

Alternatively the risen dough may be halved and rolled out like pastry and the filling sandwiched between. Place it in a shallow baking tin and cut through into pieces before proving.

Bake at 200°C (400°F, Reg 6) for 15-20 minutes. When cool sift icing sugar over the tops.

France:
BRIOCHES

Strictly speaking many enriched yeast cakes could be called brioches: the 'family' recipe being modified for the regional variations of this sponge, the differing proportions of flour, liquid, eggs and butter making it more – or less – rich. Practice will help you to know whether you need a little more flour or liquid, depending on the size of eggs used, the quality of the flour and butter and the conditions in which you are working.

The shape of the cooking tin is often particular to the cake's name and provenance. Gugelhopf (or Koughof and all similar spellings) is Austrian or German, baked in a deep elaborate mould with a centre funnel. Savarin from France is a soft batter, baked in a plain ring mould with a centre hole. The Italian Christmas cake Panettone Natale is a light fragrant loaf with sultanas, candied and fresh citrus peel, vanilla scented with a high domed top, shiny with egg glaze and baked in a thick collar of greaseproof paper. All these and more are first or second cousins in the yeast cake family.

Plain brioches should be baked in fluted tins, well buttered to prevent sticking, with a little piece of dough on the top to make a 'knob'. The result is improved if you stand the dough overnight in a cool place.

8oz (225g) wholemeal flour
½oz (12g) fresh yeast or half a sachet of either granulated or Easy-Blend dried yeast
1 tablespoon warm milk
pinch of salt
½oz (12g) sugar
2 beaten eggs
4oz (110g) melted butter

Activate the fresh or granulated yeast in the milk. If using Easy-blend yeast add it to the sifted flour with the salt and sugar. Stir all the ingredients together, then knead well, adding a little more flour if necessary to make a soft but not sticky dough. Stand it overnight if possible in a cool place, but don't refrigerate.

Knock the dough down, handling lightly. Butter the tins well and three quarters fill with the dough; for 'top knots' press a dent in the top and add a little ball of dough. Allow to prove until the dough fills the tins, bake at 230°C (450°F, Reg 8) for about 10 minutes for the small cakes, 20-25 minutes for a large one. The recipe makes up to 12 small brioches, lovely with coffee or afternoon tea.

The same recipe with 12oz (350g) of flour and only one teaspoon of sugar will give you a tender rich dough for savoury pies: an excellent dish is made by encasing an all-meat cooked continental sausage. This needs to be done whilst the meat is still warm. Allow the dough to recover from handling, then bake at 220°C (425°F, Reg 7) for 20-25 minutes. Cut into thick slices and eat whilst still warm.

SAVARIN AND RUM BABAS

These make an exotic sweet course or teatime treat. You need a ring tin for Savarin and large bun tins for individual Rum Babas. This mixture is not so much a dough as a thick batter; beat well with a wooden spoon rather than kneading it.

4oz (110g) wholemeal flour
½oz (12g) fresh yeast or half a sachet of dried yeast
pinch of salt
about 3-4 fl.oz (80ml) warm milk
1 teaspoon sugar
2oz (50g) butter, just melted
2 beaten eggs

Activate the fresh or granulated yeast in the warm milk with just a pinch of sugar until it is frothy; if using Easy-blend yeast mix it dry, with the flour. Mix all the ingredients together, beating thoroughly.

For Savarin butter a ring mould well, half fill with the batter and prove, covered with plastic film to prevent it drying, until doubled in size. Bake at 200°C (400°F, Reg 5-6) for 20-25 minutes until well risen and brown. Turn out to cool. If you have no ring mould, an ordinary round cake tin will serve for the Savarin: stand a small clean tin in the centre with a strip of greaseproof paper around it.

For Rum Babas butter large individual bun tins and place a few currants in the bottom of each. Half fill with the batter and leave to prove. Bake for about 10-12 minutes and then turn out to cool.

To finish the cakes put them back in their tins, prick them all over with a clean skewer and then pour over them a warm sugar syrup made by adding 4oz (110g) sugar to half a pint (275ml) of water and heating gently until dissolved, then boiling until syrupy. Add rum for the Rum Babas, of course! When the syrup has been absorbed, turn the cakes out onto serving dishes.

SALT DOUGH MODELLING

You can model salt dough like clay and use it to make a variety of decorative and symbolic designs for seasonal displays and celebrations. The high salt content acts as a preservative and the models will last for a long time.

Basic Dough

Use a small mug, a standard cup or a liquid measure.
- 2 measures of plain white flour
- 1 measure of salt
- less than one measure of cold water
- 1 tablespoon of glycerine will make the dough easier to handle

Mix the salt with the flour and add the water and glycerine to make a dough. Knead it until it is smooth and elastic. Wrap the dough in polythene and leave for an hour before using.

Tools Needed

- Wooden board or a plastic tray as a working surface
- Rolling pin or smooth bottle
- Small knife
- Cutters of various shapes and sizes (lids and bottle tops are useful)
- Various means of applying surface texture such as buttons, cocktail sticks, spoon handles, the tip of the knife, nuts and bolts, screws, fork prongs, a sieve, etc.
- Artist's brush for applying water Inexpensive plastic icing set will provide nozzles to extrude textured strips

Colour

You can add colour by kneading into a portion of the dough a teaspoon of cocoa, instant coffee or gravy browning. Food colourings can be used if the pieces are not going to be dried by baking. You can also develop colour by using various glazes: dissolve salt in water and paint on for white, milk will give a pale fawn and beaten egg a deep gold. Sugar dissolved in water will give shades of brown. Give several applications to give a good colour and gloss; the oven temperature will also affect the final result.

After drying or baking, decoration may be added by painting with craft enamels, poster or acrylic colours or spray paints, e.g. in gold or silver. Several coats of polyurethane varnish give a good shiny finish.

Texture

You can create designs by twisting, plaiting, using cut-outs and overlays, by pressing and by adding shredded or grated dough. After drying or baking you can use a thin layer of gum or fabric adhesive to stick on seeds, spices or glitter. You can also use silver dragees or coloured sugar strands.

Techniques

Use a dusting of flour to stop the dough sticking to working surfaces. Coil rolls for twists, plaits, balls or letters. Roll out the dough for basic plaques and cut-outs. The dough can be free-modelled for one-off pieces such as leaves and flowers, using your fingers and simple tools. If the dough cracks add just a few drops of water. If it is sticky you can add a little more flour.

Don't forget to pierce holes for hanging ribbons or cords.

Pieces of dough will stick together if one piece is lightly dampened with water and the other piece gently pressed on top. Don't flood with water or the drying times will be increased.

Drying

In air:

Lay the pieces on polythene or plastic trays (not metal as it may rust) and leave in a warm place for several days, the top of a central heating boiler is ideal. This way keeps the original shape and colour. Turn the pieces over so that the back dries as well. You need to air dry for several days before continuing to dry in the oven.

In the oven:

low temperatures are needed (an electric oven or solid fuel cooker is best as they have dry heat). Pieces up to ¼" thick will need a minimum of one hour at a very low temperature (about 75°C), then ½ hour at 100°C and then ½ hour at 125°C. The pieces should be dry, even coloured and crisp. Thicker pieces will need much longer. Leave them for longer at the lower temperature; if the oven is too hot the pieces will distort, shrink or crack. Use aluminium baking sheets dusted with flour.

Glazing

Glaze with salt, milk, egg wash or sugar solutions as mentioned earlier on. Colour will be affected by the number of applications: brush them on at 15 minute intervals increasing the temperature each time by about 10-20°C each time up to the maximum 200°C. Watch the colour carefully in the latter stages as the pieces may scorch.

Storage

The pieces should be stored in a cool and dry place, packed in plastic or cardboard boxes with paper between the layers.

CONVERSIONS: METRIC & IMPERIAL

These are approximate conversions between Imperial and Metric measurements which have been rounded up or down. Use either Imperial or Metric measures in any one recipe.

Weight

Ounces	Grammes
1	25
2	50
3	75
4	110
5	150
6	175
7	200
8	225
10	275
12	350
14	400
16	450

Fluid Measure

Fluid Ounce	Millimetres
1	25
2	50
3	75
5	150
10	300
15	400
20	570

Temperature

°C	°F	Reg	Oven
140	275	1	slow
150	300	2	slow
170	325	3	moderate
180	350	4	moderate
190	375	5	hot
200	400	6	hot
220	425	7	very hot
230	450	8	very hot
240	475	9	very hot

Measurement

Inches	Centimetres
½	1
1	2½
2	5
6	15
8	20
9	23
10	25
11	28
12	30

Temperatures for Yeast Cookery

	°C	°F
cold/cool room	10	50
slow dough rising	15	60
normal rising	21-24	70-75
dough liquor temp	37-43	98-108
human body temp	37	98
yeast is killed at...	54	130